Turbulent Planet

White-Out

Blizzards

Claire Watts

Raintree

Chicago, Illinois

For information, address the publisher:
Raintree, 100 N. LaSalle, Suite 1200, Chicago, IL 60602
Customer Service: 888-363-4266
Visit our website at www.raintreelibrary.com

Printed and bound in China by South China Printing Company.
08 07 06
10 9 8 7 6 5 4 3 2

Library of Congress Cataloging-in-Publication Data
Watts, Claire.
  White-out : blizzards / Claire Watts.
    p. cm. -- (Turbulent planet)
  Includes bibliographical references and index.
  ISBN 1-4109-1101-2 (lib. bdg.) -- ISBN 1-4109-1208-6 (pbk.) 1.
Blizzards--Juvenile literature. I. Title. II. Series.
  QC926.37.W38 2004
  551.55'5--dc22

                          2004014648

Photo acknowledgments
The publishers would like to thank the following for permission to reproduce photographs: p.4/5, Corbis/Benjamin Lowy; p.5 top, Science Photo Library/Micheal Marten; p.5 middle, Corbis Sygma/The Scotsman; p.5 bottom, Science Photo Library/Alan & Sandy Carey; p.6/7, Corbis/Warren Morgan; p.6 Corbis/Kevin Fleming; p.8/9, Corbis/Randy Faris; p.8, Corbis/Jim Zuckerman; p.10/11, Corbis/Richard Hamilton Smith; p.10, Science Photo Library/Dr Juan Alean; p.11 Science Photo Library/W Bacon; p.12, Frank Lane Picture Agency; p.13, Photodisc; p.13 right, Corbis/Niall Benvie; p.14, Premium Stock; p.14 left, Corbis/Steve Terrill; p.15 Corbis/Bill Ross; p.16/17, Corbis/Doug Wilson; p.16, Corbis/Christopher J Morris; p.17, Corbis/Brooks Kraft; p.18/19, Corbis/Bettmann; p.18, Corbis/Karl Weatherly; p.19, Corbis/Bettmann; p.20/21 Corbis/James L Amos; p.20, Corbis/David Pollack; p.21, Corbis/Chuck Keeler Jr; p.22/23, Corbis/Reinhard Eisle; p.22, Corbis/John Noble; p.23, Corbis/Julie Habel; p.24, Science Photo Library/ Philippe Psaila; p.25, Corbis/Julie Habel; p.26/27, Corbis/ Ecoscene/Nick Hawkes; p.26, Science Photo Library/David Ducross; p.27, Science Photo Library/Micheal Marten; p.28/29, Corbis/Micheal Boys; p.28, Discovery Picture Library; p.29, Corbis/Paul Almasy; p.30/31, Discovery Picture Library; p.30, Corbis/James Leynse; p.31, Corbis/ Jack Fields; p.32, Galen Rowell; p.32 left, Galen Rowell; p.33, Corbis Sygma/The Scotsman; p.33 right, Corbis/Peter Harholdt; p.34/35, Corbis/Wolfgang Kaehler; p.34, Corbis/ Lowell Georgia; p.36/37 Corbis Sygma/Tiroler Tageszeitung/Thomas Boehm; p.36, Frank Lane Picture Agency/Jim Reed; p.37, Corbis/Doug Wilson; p.38, Frank Lane Picture Agency/Jim Reed; p.39, Corbis/Lowell Georgia; p.39 right, Linpac Environmental Ltd; p.40/41, Corbis/Picimpact; p.40, Science Photo Library/Mark Clarke; p.41, Science Photo Library/Alan & Sandy Carey; p.42/43, Frank Lane Picture Agency/Jim Reed; p.42, Science Photo Library/ David Vaughan; p.43, Science Photo Library/Micheal Marten

Cover photograph reproduced with permission of Camera Press.

Every effort has been made to contact copyright holders of any material reproduced in this book. Any omissions will be rectified in subsequent printings if notice is given to the publishers.

Disclaimer
All the Internet addresses (URLs) given in this book were valid at the time of going to press. However, due to the dynamic nature of the Internet, some addresses may have changed, or sites may have changed or ceased to exist since publication. While the author and publishers regret any inconvenience this may cause readers, no responsibility for any such changes can be accepted by either the author or the publishers.

The paper used to print this book comes from sustainable resources.

Contents

Any words appearing in the text in bold, **like this,** are explained in the glossary. You can also look out for them in the "Stormy Words" box at the bottom of each page.

Snow as Far as You Can See

Sudden change

The sky darkens as the storm clouds begin to gather. A few large snowflakes **drift** down, then more and more fall. A howling wind whips the flakes around. The air is full of swirling snow. You cannot even see your hand in front of your face.

White-out

A blizzard is not just a heavy fall of snow. A fierce wind blows the snow around in the air, too. A very bad blizzard is called a **white-out.** This is when you feel as if you are surrounded in whiteness. A storm like this could last for a few hours or for days.

Dangerously cold

Icy cold winds and heavy snow together make conditions very dangerous for people. The temperature can fall to -13 °F (-25 °C) or lower. People may die from **exposure** to the bitter cold.

exposure   being unprotected from the weather
landmark   part of the surrounding area that is easy to recognize

White-outs bring more dangers. A person in a blizzard cannot see **landmarks**. Some people have been lost in the snow for days because they could not see where to go.

When at last the blizzard dies down, the dangers are not over. The **freezing** temperatures are still deadly, and some land lies buried under feet of snow. Cars, people, and animals can easily become stuck in deep **snowdrifts**.

Find out later . . .

How do you know a blizzard is coming?

What sort of clothing is best in a blizzard?

Why are dogs useful after a blizzard?

snowdrift   deep pile of snow. The snow is piled up by the wind.
white-out   extreme blizzard. You cannot see anything in a white-out.

What Is a Blizzard?

So what is the difference between a snowstorm and a blizzard? A snowstorm is a heavy fall of snow. Snow **drifts** when the winds get stronger than 30 miles (48 kilometers) per hour. A blizzard is a **severe** snowstorm with winds of over 32 miles (51 kilometers) per hour. The worst blizzards happen when winds reach 45 miles (72 kilometers) per hour or more. Then the **visibility** is zero.

Blowing snow

Blizzards can even happen when snow is not falling. Snow can sometimes lift back into the air if a strong wind blows across it. The wind may blow the snow up to 330 feet (100 meters) high. This is as high as a 30-story building. It is impossible to tell if it is actually snowing or not.

Snowrollers

When the wind blows fresh snow along the ground, the snow can stick together. It forms a huge snowball, called a snowroller. The snowroller gathers snow as it rolls along the ground. Snowrollers can grow to about 5 feet (1.5 meters) in diameter.

△ This is Mount Everest, Tibet. The wind blows the tiny **particles** of snow into the air, making a snow **plume.**

continent   large area of land surrounded by sea
hemisphere   half of Earth. There is a northern and a southern hemisphere.

Where in the world?

Blizzards are a regular winter danger for some people. These severe snowstorms usually happen in the middle of large **continents** in the northern **hemisphere,** such as North America, Europe, and Asia. Winter temperatures are always very low in these areas. The air is also very dry because it is a long way from the sea. These are the perfect conditions for blizzards.

Mountain snow

Blizzards often occur high up in mountains. The air is extremely cold. The strong mountain winds whip the snow around in the **freezing** air.

This map shows the places mentioned in this book. The areas blizzards are most likely to occur are shown in gray. These are in the middle of large continents in the northern hemisphere. ▽

particle tiny part of something
visibility distance you can see

How snow falls

To understand how blizzards happen, first, you need to take a closer look at snow.

Inside the clouds, **water vapor condenses** around tiny specks of dust, salt, and chemicals. It **freezes** to form ice **crystals.** The ice crystals stick together, and they then grow into snowflakes. When the snowflakes are too heavy to stay in the air, they fall to the ground.

Some snowflakes form amazingly beautiful star shapes, while others form needles, blocks, or columns. Most have six sides or points. The size and shape of a snowflake affects how fast it can fall through the air.

It is easy to see the six points of these enlarged snowflakes. ▽

A gust of wind easily lifts the dry ▷ snow off these rocks and into the air. The wind also blows dust around like this during a duststorm.

condense   when a vapor or a gas turns into a liquid
crystal   solid with tiny bits arranged in a regular pattern

Wet snow

There is more water vapor in the air when the temperature is only just below the **freezing point.** This vapor freezes into many ice crystals. These ice crystals join together to form large snowflakes. This type of snow is called wet snow. Wet snow is too heavy to blow far in the wind. It makes a thick blanket of snow, with hardly any air in it.

Dry snow

The air has very little water vapor in it when the temperature is well below the freezing point, and the snowflakes stay very small. This type of snow is light and powdery. It is known as dry or powder snow. It can easily be blown by the wind. This is the type of snow found in a blizzard.

Snowflake facts

The largest snowflakes ever recorded were 5 inches (12.5 centimeters) across. The tiniest snowflakes measure less than 0.02 inches (0.5 millimeters). They are known as diamond dust.

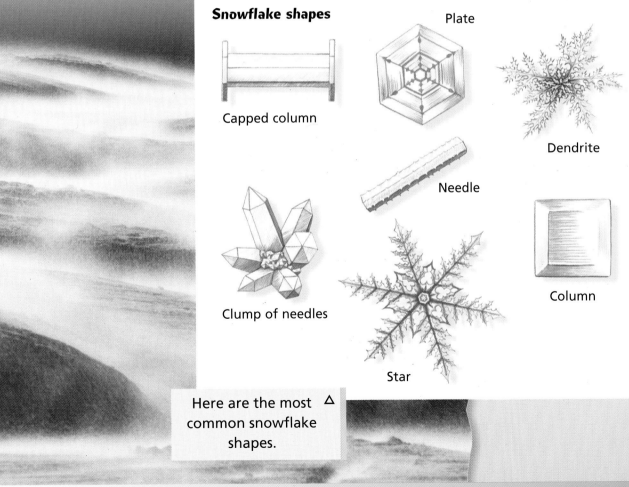

Snowflake shapes

Capped column

Plate

Dendrite

Needle

Clump of needles

Column

Star

Here are the most common snowflake shapes. △

freeze   when a liquid changes into a solid. Water freezes at 32 °F (0 °C).
water vapor   water in the form of a gas

A hidden landscape

Blizzards fill in the gaps in the land with snow. The actual shape of the land is hidden. The wind builds snow up into amazing shapes, such as waves or **cornices.** The landscape completely changes.

Snowdrifts

When the wind blows the snow against a building or a fence, the snow piles up. This forms a **snowdrift.** One side of a building could be buried under deep snow, while the other side might be completely bare. The wind can pack the snow down hard, making it difficult to dig out later. During a blizzard, the wind sometimes changes direction. First, a huge snowdrift is built up. Then, it is swept away.

◁ Sometimes the wind blows the snow into an overhanging ledge called a cornice.

The wind can sweep the ▷ snow into patterns. They look like waves.

Avalanche

When deep snowdrifts form on a mountain, **avalanches** are a real danger. Huge areas of soft snow can suddenly break away and slide down the mountain. The falling snow sweeps people or animals along with it. An avalanche can bury or even crush a building in its path. People sometimes set off explosions in the mountains to make the loose snow fall away. It then never becomes thick enough to cause a **severe** avalanche.

How avalanches happen

Most avalanches occur in spring. The air becomes warmer, and the snow starts to thaw and crack. The snow below a crack may fall away down the mountain, gathering more snow as it goes. An avalanche may reach a speed up to 250 miles (400 kilometers) per hour.

True or false?

A loud noise can set off an avalanche.

Answer: True.

Sound waves from a loud noise such as a gunshot can sometimes disturb loose snow and set off an avalanche.

△ An avalanche pours down Mount McKinley in Alaska.

cornice   overhanging ledge of snow

Blizzards in the Wilderness

When a blizzard whips across the frozen land of Siberia or the Canadian Rocky Mountains, it probably will not make the news. Hardly anyone lives in the wilderness, and the animals and plants can cope with the icy winds and **snowdrifts.**

Fur and feathers

Animals such as deer and stoats grow thick coats in winter. These protect them from freezing temperatures and the blizzard winds. In the Rocky Mountains in North America, the snowshoe hare grows thick fur on its feet. This keeps its feet warm and helps it to hop across the snow's surface without sinking. Some birds fluff out their feathers to trap a layer of warm air next to their bodies.

Warm and cozy

When blizzards sweep across the land, snow covers up plants and water **freezes.** Animals have very little to eat and drink. Some animals, such as mice, chipmunks, and insects, **hibernate** in winter. They make themselves a warm nest and their breathing slows down. Some larger animals, such as bears, also hibernate.

△ Emperor penguin chicks huddle together to keep each other warm in the snow.

frostbite   injury caused by parts of the body being frozen
hibernate   spend the winter in a very deep sleep

Winter stores

Other animals, such as squirrels, gather food in the fall. Although they spend most of the winter sleeping, from time to time they wake up to eat their stored food.

The porcupine's thick, long, stiff hairs trap air to help keep it warm. ▽

Wind chill

The wind can make the air feel colder than it really is. This effect is called wind chill. If the air temperature was -9 °F (-23 °C) and a 25 miles (40 kilometers) per hour wind was blowing, it would feel like -60 °F (-51 °C) to people and animals. When it is very cold, people begin to suffer from **hypothermia** and **frostbite**.

This red squirrel buries nuts in the fall. When the winter comes, it searches for its stored food. ▷

hypothermia   medical condition caused by being too cold

Made for snow

Many plants found in places with heavy snow and blizzards have very short stems. This stops strong winds from breaking or uprooting them. Trees grow in these areas, too. They are mostly **evergreens** and have springy branches. These can bend under the weight of snow and the force of the wind. Snow also slips off their needles easily.

Amazing but true

Snow can actually keep the ground underneath warm. During the winter of 1891 in Devon, United Kingdom, wheat **germinated** and grew to 3 inches (7.5 centimeters) beneath the snow.

△ An iris grows through the snow-covered ground.

deciduous   describes a tree that sheds its leaves in winter
evergreen   describes a tree that keeps its leaves all year round

Blanket of snow

A blizzard leaves a blanket of snow over the ground, covering up the plants. The snow protects some of the plants underneath from **freezing** winds. Cold winters kill many plants altogether. These plants leave their seeds in the soil. In spring, the seeds grow quickly. Shoots appear as soon as the snow begins to melt. Tiny wild flowers may even blossom before the snow has gone.

Snow on Mount Shasta, △ California.

Ice, but no water

Most of the water in the ground is frozen during winter. Plants and trees cannot take the water up through their roots, but they still lose water through their leaves into the air. When the blizzard winds blow, plants lose water even more quickly. Plants will die if they keep losing water without being able to replace it.

How do plants cope with this? **Deciduous** trees lose their leaves in winter completely. Evergreen trees have tough, waxy leaves. These lose very little water and stay on the tree throughout winter.

It's a record

The largest amount of snow ever to fall in a single snowstorm was 190 inches (480 centimeters) at Mount Shasta, California, in February 1959.

germinate   begin to grow from a seed

The Blizzard Strikes

When winter storms damage power lines, people can be trapped in their homes without heat and light. ▽

Blizzard hazards: Hypothermia

People's normal body temperature is 98.6 °F (37 °C). When it drops below this, people start to suffer from **hypothermia**. Their breathing and blood flow slows down. They begin to mumble and stumble. They may either shiver or their muscles could stiffen up. If their body temperature falls below 81 °F (27 °C), they will die.

Our modern world is filled with things to make our lives easier. We can create light when it is dark, travel huge distances very quickly, and find food at any time. But, when a blizzard hits a **populated** area, it is a different matter.

Complete standstill

Heavy snowfall and poor **visibility** can stop all forms of transportation. Road and rail traffic may be **stranded** in **snowdrifts.** Airports close in a blizzard because airplanes cannot take off or land safely in blowing snow. Planes already in the air will be **diverted** to another airport until the storm is over.

Power cuts

Strong winds may blow down power and telephone poles. Heavy ice can break the cables. Homes and businesses will be left without electricity or telephones until the lines can be repaired.

diverted   sent to a different place
populated   where people live together in the same area

No school, no work

Schools and workplaces will close early or not open at all. People can then stay safely in their homes rather than risk getting caught in the blizzard. If a storm blows up suddenly when people are at school or work, they could be stuck there until the blizzard ends. When deliveries cannot reach stores and gas stations for just a day or two, supplies begin to run out. Factories and businesses cannot operate for long without deliveries, either.

Snow makes road travel very dangerous. The police are often called out to deal with road ◁ accidents during snowstorms.

March 15, 1993

Superstorm Hits U.S.

For three days, a **severe** blizzard has battered the east coast of the United States, creating drifts up to 33 ft (10 m) deep. Transportation is at a standstill and all major airports have been closed. Around 270 people may have died in some of the worst weather in American history.

Snowplows struggle to clear the ▷ snow at an airport in Boston, Massachusetts.

snowplow   vehicle that clears snow from the road
stranded   stuck in a difficult situation

One step at a time

Just being outside can be dangerous during a blizzard. It is easy to get lost when you cannot see through the snow. Wading through deep, soft snow is tiring, especially if the wind is blowing straight at you. You might fall into a **snowdrift** while the icy wind chills your body.

Most people try to stay in a sheltered place during a blizzard, but this is not always possible. Explorers and soldiers may find themselves far from shelter when a blizzard strikes.

Napoleon's defeat

In 1812 France was at war with Russia. When the Russian winter closed in, the French emperor, Napoleon, told his troops to **retreat** to France. They marched through blizzards and deep snow. Soldiers **collapsed** from hunger and **exhaustion** and **froze** to death where they lay. Out of 600,000, only 100,000 returned. They were not defeated by the Russian army, but rather by the Russian winter.

Blizzard hazards: Snow blindness

When the sun's rays reflect off snow and ice, people can become blinded by the **glare**. If they cover their eyes with a blindfold, their sight gradually returns. The best way to avoid snow blindness is to wear goggles or sunglasses, like this skier.

△ These German soldiers huddle close together to keep warm in the deep Russian snow during 1941–43.

collapse fall down
exhaustion extreme tiredness

Hitler's troops freeze

Germany invaded Russia in the summer of 1941, during World War II. When winter came, the temperatures fell to around -40 °F (-40 °C). The German troops did not have good winter clothing. They had to take snowsuits and overboots from the dead bodies of Russian soldiers. The Russians had the right equipment to fight in extreme winter conditions. The Germans were driven out of Russia in 1943.

Blizzard blow

British explorer Robert Falcon Scott and his team got to the South Pole, Antarctica, on January 17, 1912. But they were not the first. A Norwegian, Roald Amundsen, beat them to it by about five weeks. Scott's team was hit by terrible blizzards on the return journey, and all five died. Antarctica is widely known as the home of the blizzard.

△ Scott's team, (from left to right) Lawrence Oates, Henry Bowers, Robert Falcon Scott, Edward Wilson, and Edgar Evans.

glare   painfully bright light
retreat   go back

◁ Road signs may become hidden by heavy snow.

True or false?

Roads are most slippery when they are covered with thick snow.

Answer: False.

Roads are more slippery with just a thin layer of snow. As the snow gets thicker, tires grip the snow more easily. But the tires may sink into the soft snow.

Road closed

You are in the car when the wind begins to whip up the snow. Gradually, the wipers clear a smaller and smaller gap on the windshield. You cannot see the other vehicles on the road or even where the edges of the road are. You must find a safe place to stop until the blizzard ends.

Lost in the snow

One of the most dangerous places to be when a blizzard strikes is in a car, out on the road. **Drifting** snow can hide dangers on the roads, such as rocks or fallen trees. The snow hides **landmarks** and covers road signs.

convoy   group of vehicles traveling together for safety
exhaust   waste gases that come out of an engine

What to do if your car gets stuck in a blizzard

o Stay in the car.
o Tie brightly colored cloth to the antenna.
o Start the car and use the heater for ten minutes every half hour.
o Keep the **exhaust** pipe clear.
o Keep one window slightly open to let air in.
o Move your arms and legs to keep warm.
o Do not fall asleep.

Skidding

It is difficult to drive in any snow, but roads are most slippery as snow begins to fall. Tires are more likely to slide on a thin layer of snow than a thick layer. To avoid a skid, you should drive very slowly. Cars and trucks cause more problems when they skid.

If you have to drive through a **snowdrift,** the car must travel fast enough to push the snow away, but slowly enough for it not to skid.

△ Traffic slows to walking speed as the road becomes slippery.

Stranded

As a blizzard becomes fiercer, drivers may become **stranded** in their vehicles. **Snowplows** will need to battle through the snow to clear a **route** for them. Police **four-wheel drive** vehicles can sometimes escort a **convoy** of trapped vehicles to safety.

---

four-wheel drive   vehicle in which the engine turns all four wheels
route   roads you would take to travel from one place to another

Down on the farm

A sudden blizzard can leave farm animals cut off in the fields without food or water. Cattle can nuzzle through snow about 6 inches (15 centimeters) deep to reach grass to eat, but they cannot push aside deeper snow.

Animals often walk with their backs to the wind until they reach a fence or a wall. The snow builds up against the barrier if the wind continues to blow in the same direction. The snow will bury the animals, and they may **freeze** to death.

These sheep in the Alps have found a patch of bare grass to graze. They have flocked together to keep each other warm.

Huddling together

Herds of sheep or cattle huddle together to protect each other from the cold. Once the animals in the center of the group are warm, they move to the edge to give others a chance to warm up.

January 19, 1982

Sheep Rescue

In the United Kingdom, a Cotswold farmer thought he had lost his flock of sheep in last week's blizzard. Rescuers found three sheep still alive under a 16.5-foot (5-meter) **snowdrift**. They had spent twelve days buried in the snow. The farmer was amazed and relieved.

Snow caves

Sheep can live for several weeks in snow-covered country. Their woolly coats keep them warm, and they are able to nuzzle through deep snow to reach the grass. When snow completely covers a sheep, the warmth from its body melts the snow around it. This forms a small cave. Sheep may even give birth to lambs inside these snow caves. However, sometimes when the snow begins to melt, the animals drown in the water.

Lifeline

If you have to go outside the house during a blizzard, tie one end of a long rope to the house and the other end to your body. You will then always find your way back to the house.

Blizzard hazards: Suffocation

Tiny **particles** of fine snow may fill the lungs of people and animals as they breathe. This can cause them to **suffocate**. Covering your mouth and nose with a scarf will protect you from the snow.

Predicting Blizzards

Being prepared for a blizzard can make the difference between life and death. Weather scientists, called **meteorologists,** watch out for signs of blizzards.

It is very hard to **predict** exactly what the weather will do. Meteorologists cannot be certain if a storm will be a huge blizzard or a small snowstorm. The wind could even change direction suddenly and blow the storm somewhere else.

Weather warnings

Warnings are **broadcast** on television, radio, and the Internet. The first warning says that a storm might be coming your way. You must keep checking the weather **forecast** if you hear a weather warning.

◁ This scientist is taking measurements of the snow. Studying snow will help scientists to find new ways to predict blizzards.

Warning	Snow	Wind	Visibility
Heavy snow	More than 1.6 in. (4 cm) deep	Less than 32 mi (51 km) per hour	More than 492 ft (150 m)
Drifting snow or blizzards	Heavy snow	Over 32 mi (51 km) per hour	492 ft (150 m) or less
Very heavy snow or severe blizzards	More than 5.9 in. (15 cm) deep	Over 45 mi (72 km) per hour	Near zero

broadcast   give out information on the radio, television, or the Internet
forecast   news that predicts something that might happen

Severe weather warning

When meteorologists are certain that the storm is heading to your area, you will hear a **severe** weather warning. This tells you when to expect the storm and how strong it will be.

Weather signs

Before radio and television, people had no warnings about the weather. They would look for signs from nature to tell them if a cold winter was coming. For example, animals might grow their winter coats earlier than usual. However, until the skies clouded over and the winds began to howl, people did not know a blizzard was on its way.

BLIZZARD DIARY

Day 1

Everyone cheered when they told us we were going home because a blizzard was coming. The school buses were there already, but some kids had to wait for their parents. I hope they all got home safely. When the bus reached my house, there was a huge black storm cloud covering the sky.

If you do not take notice of blizzard warnings, you could get stuck in the snow, like this school bus. ▷

meteorologist   person who studies, forecasts, and reports the weather
predict   say or guess that something will happen

Signs in the sky

There are weather stations all over the world. Some are on aircraft, high up in mountains, or on ships out at sea. They record temperature, **air pressure**, cloud patterns, and the speed and direction of wind.

Looking down from space

Up in space, **weather satellites** send pictures of clouds, temperature measurements, and other weather information back to Earth. Some satellites circle around Earth, giving a complete view of our planet. Others stay above one point on Earth's surface, in order to record the weather in one area.

All this information gives us a picture of what the weather is like at the moment. How can **meteorologists** use this to figure out what the weather is going to be like tomorrow or next week?

◁ This drawing is of a weather satellite positioned above Africa and Europe. It sends information back to Earth every 30 minutes.

air pressure   force of air pressing down on Earth
current   flow of air or water

Blizzard warning

Meteorologists compare the new information and weather patterns with those they have recorded before. For example, meteorologists' measurements might show there is a warm air **current** from the south moving toward a cold air current from the north. They know these weather patterns could cause a snowstorm or a blizzard.

Snow clouds
These clouds may bring heavy snow.

Cumulonimbus:
Heavy cloud with towering shape, base often very dark.

◁ An open spot with no buildings or trees around is a good site for a weather station.

Planning for Winter

Blizzard supplies

- ✓ First-aid kit
- ✓ Battery-powered radio
- ✓ Flashlight
- ✓ Extra batteries
- ✓ Candles
- ✓ Camping stove and fuel
- ✓ Matches
- ✓ Canned food
- ✓ Can opener
- ✓ Bottled water
- ✓ Extra warm clothing

At the start of winter, across North America, northern Europe, and Asia, people prepare for the blizzard season. They make sure their homes, especially pipes, are **insulated** against the cold. When water **freezes,** it **expands** and can burst pipes. People stock up on supplies of food and water. Power could be cut off for a long time. In case this happens, they store oil, flashlights, and candles for lighting; camping stoves for cooking; and wood or oil fires for heating.

When a blizzard is **forecast,** farmers move their animals into barns and make sure there is plenty of food and water for them.

Fruit and vegetables can be △ preserved with vinegar, alcohol, or sugar to make them last throughout the winter.

expand   increase in size
insulated   built so that the warmth cannot escape

Snug and warm

If people make all these preparations, they are ready to stay indoors when a blizzard hits. **Remote** houses may be snowed in for some time, so people need to use their supplies carefully to make sure they do not run out. Before **snowplows** were used to clear the roads, people who were snowed in by a blizzard had to wait for the snow to melt. It could be months before they could reach a town.

Winter stores

In the past, people spent the fall preparing enough food to last them through the winter. To keep their food good to eat for such a long time, they dried and salted meat and **preserved** fruit and vegetables.

Overhanging roofs

In places such as Switzerland, where heavy snow falls in winter, houses are built with overhanging roofs. This means that if snow slides off the roof, it cannot fall near enough to block doors and windows.

preserve   keep food from going bad
remote   far away from other buildings

Safety on the roads

When a blizzard is **forecast,** special trucks spread salt and gravel on the roads. Snowflakes melt when they fall onto salt. Gravel helps car tires grip the road when it is slippery with snow and ice.

In places where a lot of snow falls each year, the edges of the road are often marked with tall posts in bright colors. These stick up out of **snowdrifts** so that drivers can tell where the edges of the road are.

Blizzard hazards: Carbon monoxide poisoning

Deadly **carbon monoxide** gas comes out of the car's **exhaust.** The signs of carbon monoxide poisoning are a headache, dizziness, or drowsiness. Keep a window slightly open so fresh air can come into the car. Keep checking the exhaust pipe to make sure it is not blocked with snow.

△ Snowplows can clear snow from the road, but cars parked at the side may take longer to move.

antifreeze   liquid used to stop the water in a car's radiator from freezing
carbon monoxide   poisonous gas in car exhaust fumes

Get ready

Drivers prepare their cars for winter by changing to special winter tires or attaching snow-chains to the tires. These help the tires grip the road better. People fill up the fuel tank of the car regularly, to make sure there is no danger of running out of gas in the snow. Just in case the car does get stuck, drivers keep some emergency supplies in the trunk.

Go!

If you hear a blizzard warning and you are in a car, you should turn back or find shelter until the storm is over. If you must travel in a blizzard, it is safest to go in the daylight. You should let someone know your **destination,** your **route,** and when you expect to arrive. Then if you get stuck and do not arrive on time, you can be rescued.

Emergency supplies for the car

- ✓ Shovel
- ✓ Sand
- ✓ Tow rope
- ✓ **Jumper cables**
- ✓ Antifreeze
- ✓ Warning light or flares
- ✓ Compass
- ✓ Extra clothing and boots
- ✓ Flashlight
- ✓ Blanket or sleeping bag
- ✓ First-aid kit
- ✓ Matches
- ✓ Candle
- ✓ Emergency food
- ✓ Cell phone
- ✓ Water

◁ A truck spreads gravel and salt on the roads.

These men are fitting ▷ snow-chains to their tires. Then they can drive on deeper snow.

destination   place you are going to
jumper cables   electrical cables used for starting a vehicle engine

Protecting Yourself

Keeping warm

If you live in **freezing** winter temperatures, you have to protect yourself from the cold. The **Inuit** people of the Arctic have the perfect solution. They wear loose coats called **parkas** made out of thick **caribou** fur. The parkas are easy to move around in and trap warm air next to the wearer's body.

No sweat

In the past, when explorers and mountaineers traveled to very cold places, they wore heavy, **waterproof** clothing. Sweat and **condensation** built up under their clothes and froze, making them cold and uncomfortable. Modern cold weather clothing stops water from coming in, but allows **water vapor** out, so the body will stay dry and warm.

△ These Inuit people are wearing traditional fur parkas.

caribou   Arctic deer similar to reindeer
condensation   water droplets formed when air containing water vapor cools

Many layers of thin clothing are warmer than one thick garment. The layers trap air next to the skin and it warms up. Outer garments should have drawstrings or elastic at the openings to stop cold air and snow from getting in.

Warm head

Most body heat is lost through the head and parts of the body farthest from the heart, such as the hands and feet. It is very important to keep these parts warm in freezing conditions—or you could get **frostbite.** You should wear a hat and a hooded coat. Waterproof boots and several pairs of thick socks will keep your feet warm

This mountain rescue team is wearing waterproof clothing. The bright colors make sure they can be seen easily in the snow. ▽

Snow goggles

The Inuit used to make snow goggles from strips of bark or bone, such as the ones below. They cut narrow slits in them to look through. These goggles helped reduce the **glare** of the sun on the snow. Modern goggles have special **tinted** lenses to do this. The sun's glare can cause snow blindness.

Inuit   people who live in the Arctic
parka   fur jacket with a hood

Finding shelter

You must find shelter quickly if you get caught in a blizzard. You could find shelter in a gas station, a restaurant, or a hotel, if you are traveling. The snow might force you to stay at school, at work, or in your own home. You could even take shelter in a barn or shed.

A natural shelter

You need to find a place to get out of the wind if there are no buildings around. Look for a natural shelter, such as a wall or a cave. You should avoid places where snow might build up into **snowdrifts** or where snow might fall on you.

A snowdrift has blocked ▽ this door.

BLIZZARD DIARY

Day 2
The snow has **drifted** up against the front door, so we can't get out of the house at all. I wouldn't want to, anyway. The wind is roaring and the snow is swirling outside. It's snug in here by the fire, playing games and reading books by candlelight.

△ During an Arctic blizzard, a skilled **Inuit** hunter can build an igloo in about an hour. The igloo is made from blocks cut from snow. It can stand up to a blizzard far better than a modern tent.

draft   flow of air
drift   snow driven along or piled up by the wind

Building a shelter

There may be no shelter in **exposed** places like the Arctic or on mountains. People **stranded** in such places during a blizzard will have to use the snow itself to build a shelter. It could be a hole dug in the soft snow or an **igloo** made with blocks of firm snow.

Air holes

Wherever you decide to take shelter, do not block up every hole to keep out **drafts.** Make sure there are a few gaps or holes to allow enough air in to breathe. This is especially important if you have a fire inside the shelter, because it will burn up some of the **oxygen** in the air.

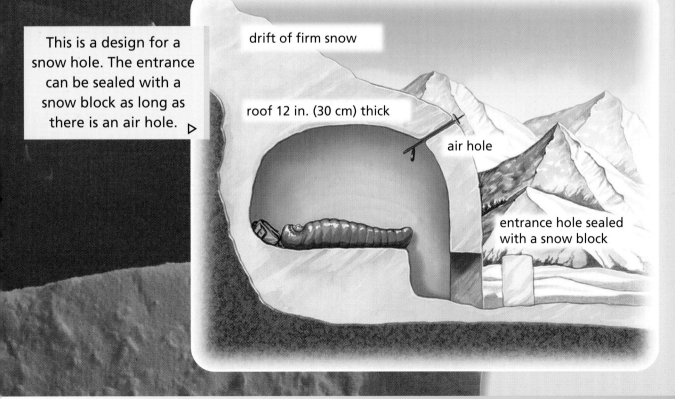

How to make a snow hole

This is a design for a snow hole. The entrance can be sealed with a snow block as long as there is an air hole. ▷

drift of firm snow

roof 12 in. (30 cm) thick

air hole

entrance hole sealed with a snow block

igloo   house made from snow blocks

After the Storm

People begin to go outside into the cold after the snow and winds die down. The first job is to dig a path from the house to the road. Shoveling snow is hard work. It is important to work slowly, or else you might suffer from **exhaustion.** From time to time you need to go inside and get warm again, before going back out into the cold.

Emergency airlift

When the snow causes houses to be **isolated** for several days, small planes or helicopters fly over and drop emergency supplies. They try to provide enough food and heating fuel to last until the roads are cleared.

BLIZZARD DIARY

Day 6

We've been trying to dig a path from the front door to the road. We took it in turns, changing over as soon as our feet and fingers started feeling numb. Even after a whole day's digging, we've only cleared about 10 feet (3 meters). I am exhausted.

△ The snow can leave isolated houses cut off from the rest of the world for days.

Even after the blizzard is over, outside it is still very cold and slippery. People should be extra careful to prevent accidents and injuries. The **emergency services** cannot easily reach places cut off by the snow. Ordinary ambulances cannot travel on snow-covered roads. The only way to get an injured person to the hospital is by helicopter.

Flood alert

The problems are still not over when the snow begins to melt. Snow can melt very quickly. The rivers and streams may become too full and burst their banks, flooding low-lying land around them.

> "
> We seemed to be the **only house in the world**, as we awoke to find our cars only barely sticking out from the **snowdrifts** and long icicles on the porch.
> "
>
> Steve Schiffres, Virginia, February 2003

△ Helicopters deliver food supplies to villages isolated by the snow.

isolated   cut off from places where people live

Clearing the roads

It takes only 4 inches (10 centimeters) of snow to make driving almost impossible in a normal car. After a blizzard, **snowdrifts** several feet thick can cover the roads. These are often completely buried. Somehow, all this snow has to be shifted.

Scraping and blowing

As soon as the wind dies down, **snowplows** can begin to help fix the mess. Snowplows scrape the snow from the road and push it to one side. They work best with wet snow because the flakes stick together and can easily be pushed into a pile.

Machines called **snowblowers** work better with dry snow. The snowblower sucks up the snow, like a vacuum cleaner, and blows it out onto the side of the road. Wet snow would stick together inside the snowblower and jam it up, but dry snow stays fine and powdery inside the machine.

This truck has a snowplow at the front and releases gravel at the back. ▷

snowblower   machine that sucks snow off the road and blows it to one side

A snowblower cuts its way through deep snow. ▽

In areas where snow is expected in△ winter, containers of gravel stand by roadsides. People can spread it on pavements and paths.

True or false

Cat litter can help you drive on snow.

Answer: True.

When a car gets stuck in snow, often the wheels cannot grip the slippery surface. Dry sand, gravel, or even cat litter in front of the wheel can help the tires to get a grip on the road, so you can drive on.

Biggest roads first

First, the snowplows clear the highways and main roads. Then, they clear smaller side roads. The very small roads in the countryside are usually cleared by the people who live on them or by farmers with tractors.

Things to remember:

- Always tell people where you are going and when you expect to be back.

- Take an experienced guide for hard walks.

To the rescue

Rescue teams search for people **stranded** outside as soon as the storm dies down. It is an urgent job. People may be buried in **snowdrifts** or **avalanches.** The rescuers need to find them before they begin to suffer from **hypothermia** or **frostbite.**

Mountain rescue

In the mountains, a blizzard can appear very suddenly, even in calm, sunny weather. People who go walking in hills or mountains should always be prepared for the weather to change. In many skiing and mountaineering areas, there are trained **mountain rescue** teams. They search for people who are lost in the snow.

◁ This **snowmobile** ambulance is used for rescuing injured skiers in the Alps.

mountain rescue　emergency service to rescue people in mountain areas
snowmobile　vehicle designed to travel through snow

The search

Rescue workers push long poles into the snow to find out if there is anything buried in it. If they touch something under the snow, they dig down carefully to find out what it is. It could be a lost person or an animal, such as a sheep.

Sniffer dogs

Rescuers often use specially trained dogs to **track** people. Dogs can search a wide area much faster than people because they have a very strong sense of smell. Dogs also walk lightly on the snow. This means the snow is less likely to collapse further onto the person. Once a dog finds someone buried in the snow, it uses its paws to help dig them out.

St. Bernard dogs

The monks at St. Bernard's monastery in the Alps sent out search parties to find lost travelers. Around 400 years ago, they started to send dogs with the search parties. The big, hairy dogs became known as St. Bernards.

A mountain rescue team pulls ◁ an injured hiker onto a sled.

track   find something by figuring out which way it went

Blizzard Survival Guide

Blizzards can kill. Fine snow combined with **freezing** winds can chill the human body in minutes. If you find yourself in an area where blizzards may strike, remember these important tips. They may help you to survive.

Weather forecasts

Check the weather **forecast** often. Leave the radio on for more information if you hear that a blizzard may be coming.

△ Scientists camping out in the Antarctic have strung up a lifeline to help them find their way around the camp in a blizzard.

Blizzard dangers

There are plenty of dangers to look out for in a blizzard situation. Here is a reminder of them.

- **Carbon monoxide** poisoning
- **Frostbite**
- **Hypothermia**
- Snowblindness
- **Suffocation**

△ A blizzard may cut off the electricity. You need to have food supplies and other sources of light and heating.

Preparation

Prepare yourself for bad weather. It can make the difference between life and death. Stock up on food and fuel at home. Always take plenty of warm clothing when you go out, even if you plan to be in the car the whole time.

Shelter

Find shelter as soon as possible if you get caught in a blizzard. Keep warm and stay out of the wind. Stay inside until the blizzard is over. Never drive in a blizzard unless you really have to.

Respect Earth's power

Modern human beings think they can control many of Earth's powerful forces. We can dam great rivers, carve tunnels through mighty mountains, and grow crops in deserts. However, there are some times when people cannot fight against Earth's power. When freezing blizzard winds howl, all you can do is sit back and wait for the storm to be over.

True or false?

Before a blizzard, the clouds are small, white, and fluffy.

Answer: False

Snow clouds are usually dark and heavy-looking. They cover the whole sky.

Find Out More

Books

Allen, Jean. *Blizzards*. Mankato, Minn: Capstone, 2001.

Murphy, Jim. *Blizzard! The Storm That Changed America*. New York: Scholastic, 2000.

Scheff, Duncan. *Nature on the Rampage: Blizzards*. Chicago: Raintree, 2003.

World Wide Web

If you want to find out more about blizzards, you can search the Internet using keywords such as these:

- blizzard +news
- snow +disasters
- winter +safety

You can also find your own keywords by using headings or words from this book. Use the search tips on the next page to help you find the most useful websites.

Organizations

The National Weather Service

An organization that keeps track of weather conditions around the country. The National weather service occasionally issues severe weather warnings when necessary. Contact them at the following address: **National Weather Service, National Oceanic and Atmospheric Administration, US Dept. of Commerce, 1325 East West Highway, Silver Spring, MD 20910 www.nws.noaa.gov**

Search tips

There are billions of pages on the Internet, so it can be difficult to find exactly what you want to find. For example, if you just type in "water" on a search engine such as Google, you will get a list of millions of web pages. These search skills will help you find useful websites more quickly:

- Decide exactly what you want to find out about first.
- Use simple keywords instead of whole sentences.
- Use two to six keywords in a search, putting the most important words first.
- Be precise. Use names of people, places, or things when you can.
- If your keywords are made up of two or more words that go together, put quote marks around them—for example, "**weather satellite.**"
- Use the "+" sign to join keywords together—for example "weather + disaster."

Where to search

Search engine

A search engine looks through millions of web pages and lists all the sites that match the words in the search box. They can give thousands of links, but the best matches are at the top of the list, on the first page. Try **google.com**.

Search directory

A search directory is more like a library of websites that have been sorted by a person instead of a computer. You can search by keyword or subject and browse through the different sites in the same way you would look through books on a library shelf. A good example is **www.yahooligans.com**.

Glossary

air pressure   force of air pressing down on Earth

antifreeze   liquid used to stop the water in a car's radiator from freezing

avalanche   large amount of snow falling down a mountain

broadcast   give out information on the radio, television, or the Internet

carbon monoxide   poisonous gas in car exhaust fumes

caribou   Arctic deer similar to a reindeer

collapse   fall down

condensation   water droplets formed when air containing water vapor cools

condense   when a vapor or a gas turns into a liquid

continent   large area of land surrounded by the sea

convoy   group of vehicles traveling together for safety

cornice   overhanging ledge of snow

crystal   solid with tiny bits arranged in a regular pattern

current   flow of air or water

deciduous   describes a tree that sheds its leaves in winter

destination   place you are going to

diverted   sent to a different place

draft   flow of air

drift   snow driven along or piled up by wind

emergency services   police, ambulance, fire, and rescue services

evergreen   describes a plant that keeps its leaves all year round

exhaust   waste gases that come out of an engine

exhaustion   extreme tiredness

expand   increase in size

exposure   being unprotected from the weather

forecast   news that predicts something that might happen

four-wheel drive   vehicle in which the engine turns all four wheels

freeze   when a liquid changes into a solid. Water freezes at 32 °F (0 °C).

freezing point   temperature at which a liquid turns into a solid

frostbite   injury caused by parts of the body being frozen

germinate   begin to grow from a seed

glare   painfully bright light

hemisphere   half of Earth. There is a northern and a southern hemisphere.

hibernate   spend the winter in a very deep sleep

hypothermia   medical condition caused by being too cold

igloo   house made from snow blocks

insulated   built so that the warmth cannot escape

Inuit   people who live in the Arctic

isolated   cut off from places where people live

jumper cables   electrical cables used for starting a vehicle engine

landmark   part of the surrounding area that is easy to recognize

meteorologist   person who studies, forecasts, and reports the weather

mountain rescue   emergency service to rescue people in mountain areas

oxygen   one of the gases in air and water that all living things need

parka   fur jacket with a hood

particle   tiny part of something

plume   cloud of powdery snow blowing from a mountain top

populated   where people live together in the same area

predict   say that something will happen

preserve   keep food from going bad

remote   far away from other buildings

retreat   go back

route   roads you would take to travel from one place to another

severe   very bad or serious

snowblower   machine that sucks snow off the road and blows it to one side

snowdrift   deep pile of snow. The snow is piled up by the wind.

snowmobile   vehicle designed to travel through snow

snowplow   vehicle that clears snow from the road

stranded   stuck in a difficult situation

suffocate   when the airways become blocked and you stop breathing

tinted   colored or darkened

track   find something by figuring out which way it went

visibility   distance you can see

waterproof   material that prevents water from passing through

water vapor   water in the form of a gas

weather satellite   weather station in space that records the weather on Earth

white-out   extreme blizzard. You cannot see anything in a white-out.

Index